The FBI and Public Corruption

By Robert Grayson

MASON CREST PUBLISHERS

Produced in association with Water Buffalo Books.
Design by Westgraphix LLC.

MASON CREST PUBLISHERS INC.
370 Reed Road
Broomall, Pennsylvania 19008
(866) MCP-BOOK (toll free)
www.masoncrest.com

Printed in the United States of America

First Printing

9 8 7 6 5 4 3 2 1

Library of Congress Cataloging-in-Publication Data

Grayson, Robert, 1951-
        The FBI and public corruption / Robert Grayson.
            p. cm. — (The FBI story)
        Includes bibliographical references and index.
        ISBN 978-1-4222-0567-9 (hardcover) — ISBN 978-1-4222-1373-5 (pbk.)
    1. United States. Federal Bureau of Investigation—Juvenile literature. 2. Corruption—
United States—Prevention—Juvenile literature. 3. Criminal investigation—United States—
Juvenile literature. I. Title.
    HV8144.F43G73 2008
    363.25'93230973—dc22   2008047903

Photo credits: © AP/Wide World Photos: cover (left), 1, 7, 12, 16, 23b, 28, 35, 41, 42, 54,
55; Department of Defense: 14; © Courtesy of FBI: cover (upper center), 26b, 33, 38, 39,
48, 51, 53, 60 (both); © Getty Images: cover (bottom center, upper right), 4b, 46; National
Archives and Records Administration: cover (bottom right), 19, 26a; Courtesy of the Prints
and Photographs Division, Library of Congress: 9, 18, 20 (both), 22, 23a; Courtesy of Richard
Nixon Presidential Library and Museum: 29; Used under license from Shutterstock Inc.: 4a,
25 (all), 40, 44.

Publisher's note:
All quotations in this book come from original sources and contain the spelling and grammatical
inconsistencies of the original text.

CONTENTS

CHAPTER 1 The Public's Enemies

Earlier, the jewelry store's clerks had put out new inventory in anticipation of holiday shoppers coming in the next day. But the store has been closed for hours now—and in the cold, quiet night, three figures make their way through a deserted alley, heading for the rear entrance of the store. Expecting to pull off a big heist, the three burglars are wearing black sweat suits to blend into the darkness and have covered their heads with black ski masks. They carry guns, ready to use them if necessary. Not far from the store, a fourth person waits in a car to help the burglars make their getaway. The crime has been well planned, the timing perfect.

Crimes involving **corruption** may take place in the open and among well-dressed men and women sitting in brightly lit offices and conference rooms. The payoff may be money handed over in an envelope, or it might be in the form of influence or power.

A Different Kind of Heist

This description of a crime in progress seems typical—committed under the cover of darkness, by masked thieves who are armed and dangerous, with a lookout stationed nearby to whisk them off before the police descend on them. Not all crimes are committed this way, however. Many crimes are committed in the bright light of day—by men or women in fashionable clothing meeting in fancy restaurants, upscale office suites, or luxury cars.

They exchange money in envelopes, shoeboxes, or paper bags. They don't carry weapons, and they make no effort to conceal their identity. These crimes are often committed in public, but few people ever notice that anything is amiss. Most often, the crime these well-heeled people are committing is buying and selling influence over major decisions. This crime is known as public corruption, and it affects millions of people.

Violating the Public Trust

The people committing these crimes hold a wide variety of jobs in local, state, and federal governments. They may be

FAST FACTS

The letters *FBI* stand for the Federal Bureau of Investigation, of course, but they also stand for the agency's motto, *Fidelity, Bravery, Integrity*, with integrity being the key word in public corruption investigations. The motto was created in 1935 by W. H. Drane Lester, editor of the Bureau's employee newsletter, *The Investigator*.

members of the U.S. Congress, state legislators, mayors, judges, building and health inspectors, even police officers. What they all have in common is a position of public trust, and they have chosen to violate that trust in exchange for money or something else of value. Those assigned to root out these corrupt officials and bring them to justice work as special agents for the Federal Bureau of Investigation (FBI).

Most public corruption takes place when public officials—elected or appointed—accept something of value from a private citizen or company, in exchange for making a favorable decision on behalf of that person or company. The item of value could be a gift, a service, a vacation, shares of stock, a share of profits in a particular enterprise, or simply cash. This crime is also known as influence peddling or bribery.

Though bribery is one of the most common violations of the public trust, it is not the only form of public corruption. Public corruption also occurs when officials **embezzle** public funds, accept **kickbacks**, fix elections, misuse a public office for personal gain, take part in political **coercion** schemes, intimidate (or bully) others, engage in **racketeering** and **extortion**, obstruct justice, or carry out **money laundering**. Sometimes these crimes are committed along with other serious offenses, including drug dealing or even murder.

Congressional Corruption

In a stunning example of public corruption, U.S. Representative James A. Traficant, Jr. (D-Ohio), was found guilty in April 2002 of demanding bribes from business executives and taking kickbacks from his own staff. One staff member testified during the trial that the representative had demanded kickbacks from him totaling $2,500 a month. Other members of Traficant's staff, who were called as witnesses, testified that the representative had instructed them to mislead the grand jury investigating him and ordered them to destroy evidence. The representative's trial became a public spectacle, as Traficant, representing himself, belittled the prosecution's case and claimed that the government had been out to get him for years. But the government case was ironclad, based on an intense, six-year investigation conducted by the FBI.

Traficant claimed that the trial was unfair, citing the government's decision not to put FBI agents who investigated the case

FAST FACTS

The FBI allocates 15 percent of its investigative resources (people, money, and equipment) to combating public corruption.

Representative James A. Traficant, Jr., of Ohio speaks with the media outside federal court in Cleveland during his trial on charges of accepting bribes and favors from businessmen. Traficant told jurors that he was an innocent victim of federal agents who hated him. The jurors rejected his argument. He was convicted of charges against him and sentenced to eight years in prison.

on the stand. He maintained that the agents weren't called to testify because the prosecution was "scared to death of my cross-examination." After the case was over, jurors said that it was obvious that Traficant was trying to confuse them. But he failed. The representative was sentenced to eight years in prison.

Former Representative Richard A. Gephardt, the Democratic leader in the House of Representatives at the time of Traficant's trial, said, "A member of Congress who commits bribery strikes at the heart of representative government."

A Long History

Public corruption has been around for as long as the world has had governments. From democracies like those found in Europe and North America to the most ruthless **dictatorships**, where almost all freedoms are denied to the citizens, government officials have been known to take bribes in exchange for granting special favors or allowing certain activities to go unreported.

At the time of the founding of the United States of America, one of the colonists' biggest complaints against the British was that many of the British officials running the 13 colonies were corrupt and that their corruption went unchecked and unpunished. After the revolution, the nation's founders made a determined effort to keep this type of corruption from tainting government in a free United States. The founders wrote safeguards into the U.S. **Constitution**, creating what is known as the system of checks and balances among the three branches of the U.S. government—legislative, judicial, and executive.

Theodore Roosevelt, president from 1901 to 1909, commented on corruption in a book of essays he wrote in 1900, saying:

> Unless a man is honest, we have no right to keep him in public life. It matters not how brilliant his capacity, it hardly matters how great his power of doing good service on certain lines may be. . . . No man who is corrupt, no man who **condones** corruption in others, can possibly do his duty by the community.

Eroding Confidence in Government

Public corruption hurts every honest person. First of all, every time a corrupt official is exposed, the public's confidence and trust in all government and all public officials are shaken as well.

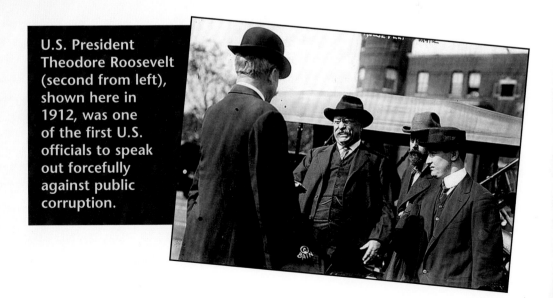

U.S. President Theodore Roosevelt (second from left), shown here in 1912, was one of the first U.S. officials to speak out forcefully against public corruption.

Corruption casts a shadow of doubt over the entire system. That is unfair to all the honest people who do uphold their oaths of office. Secondly, public corruption **undermines** the services the community is getting. If money is being diverted from a project for the personal enrichment of certain public officials, all citizens are getting less for their tax dollars. They also are getting fewer services and fewer needed improvements in their community, and that could actually slow economic growth and development in a community.

Each year public corruption results in the loss of millions of dollars, and that loss is coming right out of the taxpayers' pockets. Unearthing public corruption is a daunting task, but the FBI is well qualified to conduct these investigations, collecting the evidence needed to arrest and convict corrupt officials who betray the people they serve.

The battle to stop public corruption does not end at the nation's borders. The Foreign Corrupt Practices Act of 1977 (FCPA) was aimed at curbing the growing practice of persons from either the United States or foreign countries attempting to bribe public officials abroad to gain contracts with companies doing business with the United States. In early 2007 the FBI's assistant director, James Burrus, said this about the need to fight public corruption here and abroad:

> [O]ur highest criminal priority is to curb public corruption, whether here or overseas. It's important to consumer confidence . . . it's important to corporate competitiveness . . . and it's especially important to our democracy.

Burrus added that "companies should thrive overseas through competition, not corruption."

Beyond eroding the public trust, public corruption could potentially compromise the security of the United States. The FBI proved this point during a massive, three-year undercover sting it ran in Arizona, along border between the United States and Mexico.

Operation Lively Green started in 2002. When it was over, nearly 70 military and law enforcement members had been arrested on wide-ranging charges of extortion and bribery. Many of those arrested had accepted bribes so that smugglers could cross the southern U.S. border without interference, transporting illegal drugs, drug money,

OVER THERE!

The FBI fights international corruption, as well as domestic corruption, by using the tools it was given in the Foreign Corrupt Practices Act (FCPA) of 1977. In 2007 the FBI put together a special team of agents to handle all FCPA cases.

The special team allowed the FBI to focus on international corruption and work with other agencies investigating similar cases. The FBI also created the International Contract Corruption Task Force to crack down on corruption outside U.S. borders committed by U.S. citizens and companies. With so much U.S. industry now involved in Afghanistan, Kuwait, and Iraq, task force members are stationed there to investigate suspicious activity. But the task force's scope is not limited to those countries.

In 2006, a former executive of a company in Texas pleaded guilty to conspiracy to bribe foreign officials in order to secure construction jobs in their countries. The FBI charged that the executive gave officials in Ecuador $300,000 to get his company a contract to fix a large gas pipeline in that country. He also helped funnel a cash payment of $1.5 million to Nigerian officials for gas pipeline work there.

Corrupt deals such as these are often concealed in complicated contracts. FBI agents therefore often rely on tips from people who want to see an end to public corruption at home and abroad.

The San Ysidro Port of Entry between the United States and Mexico straddles San Diego, California, and Tijuana, Mexico. As one of the busiest border crossings in the world, San Ysidro has also become one of the most heavily monitored. Back-ups such as the one shown here have become more common as officials stay on the lookout for smugglers of arms, drugs, people, weapons, and money—all the more reason for fighting corruption among enforcement officers on both sides of the border.

and illegal immigrants. The case is one of the biggest public corruption stings in recent criminal history.

"Insulated from Political Pressure"

While the FBI's special agents have the training and skills to carry out the most delicate and sophisticated investigations, there is something even more important that gives the agency an advantage in pursuing cases of public corruption. In 2008, FBI director Robert S. Mueller III, explained what gives the agency this edge:

> The FBI is uniquely situated to address public corruption. We have the skills to conduct sophisticated

investigations. But more than that, we are insulated from political pressure. We are able to go where the evidence leads us, without fear of **reprisal** or **recrimination**.

Mueller has said on many occasions that investigating and prosecuting public corruption is a top priority of the FBI. Though the agency believes that a vast majority of public officials in the United States are honest, some public officials do violate the public trust. That's when law enforcement moves in. Said Mueller:

> For a nation built on the rule of law—and on faith in a government of the people, by the people, and for the people—we can and should do better. Ultimately, democracy and corruption cannot co-exist.

An Opening for Terrorists?

According to Director Mueller, Operation Lively Green raised the possibility of an even more dangerous scenario than the violation of public trust and the long list of crimes that were actually being committed:

> If you would sell your oath and your honor for drug money, where does one draw the line? For the right price, would such individuals permit terrorist operatives to enter the country?

Particularly since the terrorist attacks of September 11, 2001, the FBI has kept in the forefront of its investigations the added threat that public corruption could open doors for terrorists to enter the country and roam freely.

CHAPTER 2 Wayward Public Servants

Some public corruption cases get nationwide media attention; others only make the local press. The publicity one case gets doesn't make it any less important than any other case. The FBI puts in whatever hard work and determination every investigation requires, whether it involves a U.S. senator or a local health inspector.

A Zero Tolerance Policy

On August 29, 2005, Hurricane Katrina caused massive damage and loss of life to the city of New Orleans and

American soldiers ride a fan boat through the flooded streets of New Orleans, looking for survivors of Hurricane Katrina. Unfortunately, not everyone was interested in helping others. Some corrupt politicians attempted to profit from the tragedy.

surrounding communities as well as to the Gulf Coast of Mississippi and parts of Alabama. The federal government eventually sent millions of dollars in emergency aid to the area to help with cleanup and reconstruction.

With that money came the need to make sure it was used properly and to investigate any misuse of funds. Chris Swecker, assistant director of the FBI's Criminal Investigative Division at the time, said of the Bureau's mission,

> We have a responsibility to ensure that government relief efforts are not undermined by **unscrupulous** individuals. It is very unfortunate that natural disasters, such as Hurricane Katrina, while bringing out the best in most people also draw out criminal elements who would take advantage of the federal government's relief efforts.

The FBI set up a special telephone tip line in September 2005 so public corruption and fraud in connection with the Hurricane Katrina relief efforts could be reported. In December 2005, a tip came in from a Louisiana businessman under contract to serve meals at a camp that provided emergency housing to disaster relief workers helping out in New Orleans. Two Federal Emergency Management Agency (FEMA) officials at the camp had approached the businessman about engaging in a kickback scheme. The two officials offered to falsify records to inflate the number of meals the businessman's company served. In exchange, according to the plan, the contractor would give the officials some of the extra money he would be paid for meals his firm never provided.

AND THE ~~WINNER~~ LOSER IS . . .

In 2009, most people, if asked which state they thought had the highest incidence of public corruption, would probably have answered Illinois. That's because on December 9, 2008, in a highly publicized case, the FBI arrested Illinois Governor Rod Blagojevich on corruption charges related to bribery and fraud. Those charges were based on hours of secretly recorded conversations in which Governor Blagojevich was said to have attempted to "sell" political appointments and favors to the highest bidders. The most widely known accusation against the governor involved filling the U.S. Senate seat that became vacant following the election of then-Senator Barack Obama to the presidency. In January 2009, the Illinois House of Representatives voted to impeach Governor Blagojevich on the basis of various charges against him, and the Illinois Senate then tried him on those charges and voted to remove him from office. In April 2009, a federal grand jury indicted him on criminal corruption charges.

Around the same time as the FBI's arrest of Blagojevich (shown below pleading his case before the Illinois Senate), the *New York Times* published an article on public corruption in the 50 U.S. states, the District of Columbia, and three U.S. territories. The article included a "top-ten" most-corrupt list based on statistics compiled over the previous decade by the U.S. Department of Justice and Census Bureau. Many felt that the Blagojevich scandal and other well-publicized Illinois cases would certainly make Illinois statistically the most corrupt state. It was revealed, however, that Florida had the highest number of public corruption convictions, followed by New York in second place, and then Texas, Pennsylvania, California, Ohio, Illinois, New Jersey, the District of Columbia, and Louisiana. In another list, based on the number of convictions proportionate to population, the District of Columbia topped the charts. This was due, no doubt, to the large number of public officials living in a district with a relatively small general population. Rounding out this "top-ten" list were, in second place, the U.S. Virgin Islands, followed by Guam, North Dakota, Alaska, Louisiana, Mississippi, Montana, Kentucky, and Alabama.

The contractor reported the scheme to the FBI, whose agents conducted a two-month investigation that ended in the arrest of the two FEMA employees. The FBI credited the businessman for his honesty and courage in reporting the underhanded plan, which would have cost taxpayers hundreds of thousands of dollars. The two FEMA officials eventually pleaded guilty to soliciting bribes and were sentenced to prison.

Fighting Corruption and Conflict of Interest

Public corruption and **conflict of interest** among officials may seem commonplace today because the FBI has made cracking down on it such a high priority. Ever since its origins in 1908, however, the Bureau has been charged with investigating public corruption. A brief look at U.S. history reveals that corruption has been around even longer than the FBI. So have people bent on fighting it and bringing violators of the public trust to justice.

The colonial settlers in North America were well aware that political officeholders in Europe used their positions to enrich themselves. When the framers of the United States Constitution created three branches of government with separate powers and duties, they set up a system that would, they felt, help prevent corruption. At the very least, by giving each branch the power to investigate the others, such a system of checks and balances would help public officials detect corruption and root it out.

19th-Century Scandals

As the United States began to expand westward, however, opportunities for corruption grew as well, especially in local

As general in chief of the Army, Ulysses S. Grant led the Union to victory in the Civil War. His presidential administration was one of the most corrupt in U.S. history, however.

territorial governments that were awarding government contracts for construction of railroads. One of the 1800s' most corrupt presidential administrations was that of Ulysses S. Grant (1869–1877).

Grant's administration was rocked by corruption: Both his vice presidents—Schuyler Colfax in Grant's first term and Henry Wilson in his second—were accused of corrupt activities while in office. Many others in the Grant administration were forced to resign over scandals involving embezzlement and bribery. Several cabinet members had to leave office due to scandal, and despite vowing to let no guilty person escape punishment, Grant often **pardoned** those found guilty of corruption.

The biggest scandal of the Grant administration was the Crédit Mobilier scheme, which actually began in 1864, years before Grant took office. Grant himself coined the term *lobbying* to describe the actions of people who tried to advance their causes by befriending politicians. One of these *lobbyists* was Thomas Durant, an officer of the Union Pacific Railroad.

Durant created a company called Crédit Mobilier that Union Pacific hired to build a 667-mile (1,073-kilometer) stretch of railroad at an extremely inflated cost. The cost of building this railroad was paid for with money granted by the federal government. Members of Congress who helped

Union Pacific get the federal grant money for the construction of the railroad were rewarded by getting cheap stock in Crédit Mobilier. They therefore reaped financial rewards as stockholders when the company benefited from the railroad building job. Durant then hired low-paid laborers to build the railroad, at no financial risk to himself or his company, because taxpayers covered the entire cost through the federal grant. Crédit Mobilier made a reported $21 million in profit from the scheme. Durant's **cronies** in Congress each pocketed a nice sum of money.

A System That Works, but Not Very Well

The *New York Sun* newspaper reported on the scandal in 1872, during Grant's reelection bid. Grant's vice president, Schuyler Colfax, was linked to the scheme and removed from the ticket. Henry Wilson, who was also linked to the scandal, replaced Colfax, but Grant was reelected anyway.

During the 19th century, railroad work crews consisted mostly of immigrants who worked long hours for little money. Low-wage labor enabled Crédit Mobilier to make millions in profit for constructing part of the Union Pacific Railroad. Corrupt members of Congress ensured that Crédit Mobilier would receive taxpayer funds, and pocketed a share of the profit in return.

Congress investigated the Crédit Mobilier **scam** but only **censured** two of its members for the scandal. Still, the investigation did prompt Congress to pass legislation in 1876, requiring lobbyists to register with the clerk of the House of Representatives. In response, lobbyists began sneaking into the halls of Congress by pretending to be newspaper reporters. That led to reporters having to register with the clerk as well.

It was never proved that Grant was directly involved in any of the scandals during his administration. But the president was often criticized for ignoring the wrongdoing and appointing war buddies and big political contributors to jobs for which they had no qualifications.

Congress Reforms the Process

In 1883, Congress took action to reform the way people were appointed to government jobs, but it may have cost a president's life before they acted. Because Grant made cronyism—the act of appointing to government jobs friends and supporters with no qualifications—so popular, those who were denied jobs were understandably frustrated and upset.

Each vice president serving under Ulysses S. Grant—Schuyler Colfax (left) and Henry Wilson (right)—was linked to the Crédit Mobilier scandal.

President James Garfield was in office just four months when a man who was angry about not being hired for a political job in the Garfield administration shot and severely wounded the president on July 2, 1881. Garfield died of complications from the injury two months later.

Realizing that the shooting was an outgrowth of a political system that allowed officeholders to appoint unqualified people to important government jobs, Congress decided to crack down on this practice. Spurred by Garfield's assassination and the cronyism of the Grant administration, Senator George H. Pendleton (D-Ohio) proposed a law to reform the **patronage** system by establishing the federal Civil Service Commission.

Under the proposed law, which introduced the idea of merit-based hiring, prospective appointees to a job in the federal government would have to prove they were qualified to hold that job by passing a test called the civil service exam. The proposed law also protected workers from being fired because of their political leanings and made it illegal for appointees to take advantage of their government jobs to campaign for political candidates. The Pendleton Act became law in 1883, during the administration of Chester A. Arthur, who took office as president upon Garfield's death.

The Teapot Dome Scandal

One of Washington's biggest bouts with corruption took place in the 1920s. Called the Teapot Dome scandal, it was just one of many ethical missteps during the short administration of Warren G. Harding, which lasted from 1921 to 1923.

Many of the friends Harding appointed to key administration jobs were convicted of wrongdoing in various scandals

President Calvin Coolidge inherited the Teapot Dome scandal from his predecessor, Warren Harding. This political cartoon depicts anti-corruption laws and a teapot being hurled at a hat representing Coolidge's presidential campaign.

during his administration. Some even committed suicide as word of various scandals began to leak out. Teapot Dome, the most notable Harding-related scandal, was named after a Wyoming rock formation that looked like a teapot and stood over a large naval oil reserve. Even before Harding's election, the Republican National Convention that nominated him as its candidate in 1920 had been clouded by accusations that wealthy oil interests had unduly influenced his selection. Nothing was ever proved conclusively.

When Harding won the election, he appointed his close friend, Senator Albert Fall (R-New Mexico), as Secretary of the Interior in 1921. Fall quickly convinced the Secretary of the Navy to turn over to him control of the Navy's oil fields (one in Teapot Dome, Wyoming, and two in California).

Once he had control of these oil fields, Fall leased the oil fields in Teapot Dome and in Elk Hills, California, to private oil companies. These companies in turn gave Fall $400,000 for his work on their behalf. Though Fall tried to keep the deal secret, he couldn't help flaunting his new wealth. The

The close friendship of President Warren G. Harding (left; shown with his wife, Florence) and Albert B. Fall (right; first person on left) led to Harding's appointment of Hall to the position of Secretary of the Interior. It also led to the implication of Harding in the Teapot Dome scandal.

U.S. Senate and the Bureau of Investigation (now known as the FBI) started looking into the leases and Fall's role in granting them in April 1922. The full scandal was revealed to the public in 1924.

Harding died in office on August 2, 1923, as rumors of the Teapot Dome scandal were swirling around Washington, D.C. It is believed that he had a heart attack and that he was told of the details of the scandal shortly before his death. Had Harding lived, his situation would have been made worse legally by his knowledge that Harry Daugherty, the longtime friend whom he appointed as U.S. attorney general, refused to investigate the Teapot Dome scandal.

Vice President Calvin Coolidge took over for Harding and was never connected to any of his predecessor's scandals. Coolidge forced Daugherty to resign in March 1924 and

appointed a special prosecutor to investigate the
scandals of the
Harding adminis-
tration, saying,
"Let the guilty be
punished."

A Prison Term

Court action—
both criminal and
civil—followed the
work of the special
prosecutor, the Bureau
of Investigation, and the
Senate investigation of Teapot
Dome. In 1927, the U.S. Supreme Court ruled that the oil
leases the private oil companies had acquired were "null
and void"—invalid—because they had been obtained
through corruption. In 1929, Fall was finally convicted in
criminal court of taking bribes and sentenced to a year in
prison and a $100,000 fine. He became the first former
presidential cabinet member to go to prison. The oil fields
were eventually given back to the Navy.

Such widespread bribery, influence peddling, and cronyism at the highest levels of government proved the need
for an impartial, incorruptible agency to investigate these
charges and arrest those involved, no matter who they were
or who they knew. The FBI was assigned this responsibility.

FAST FACTS

Among the movies
that spotlight public corruption
are *All the King's Men* (starring
Broderick Crawford), *The Seduction
of Joe Tynan* (starring Alan Alda), *All
the President's Men* (starring Dustin
Hoffman and Robert Redford),
Mr. Smith Goes to Washington
(starring Jimmy Stewart),
and *Blaze* (starring
Paul Newman).

3 Here Come the Feds!

The federal Division of Investigation (DOI), later to become known as the FBI, came into existence in 1908. It went through some difficult growing pains, however. The very idea of establishing a federal investigative agency was controversial at first, but the American public eventually accepted the agency and its mission. In 1908, few crimes were considered violations of federal law, so the agency's impact was limited.

Helping Out the Locals

Slowly, Congress started passing laws that gave the DOI more power and the tools it needed to chase criminals who evaded local and state laws simply by crossing state lines and fleeing to another state. One of those tools was the National Motor Vehicle Theft Act of 1919, which made it a federal crime to take a stolen car from one state to another.

For most travelers, seeing one of these road signs may mean getting closer to home or to a vacation spot. For others, crossing a state line in a stolen car or in order to flee the police might mean having to deal with the FBI.

Officers in Detroit break up a secret brewing operation in the 1920s (left). During Prohibition, federal agents fought gangsters like Al Capone (right). They also fought corrupt officials who could be bribed into ignoring the illegal sale of alcohol.

This legislation gave the agency the power to pursue law-breakers across state lines and arrest them if the suspects made their getaway in a stolen car. At the time many criminals stole cars and fled to another state to evade local authorities. The local police could not cross state lines to make an arrest. With this new federal law, however, the DOI could.

In 1920, laws were passed in the United States making it illegal to sell or consume alcohol. For the next 13 years, the agency dealt with public corruption, as it fought gangsters who violated the ban on selling alcohol during Prohibition. Many of those gangsters, such as Al Capone and Dutch Schultz, carried out their illegal acts with the knowledge and even protection of public officials. Officials who publicly denounced the use of alcohol sometimes took bribes in exchange for ignoring the activities of gangsters.

Battling Racketeering

During World War II and immediately afterwards, the Bureau focused its efforts on domestic intelligence gathering. Toward the end of the 1950s and the beginning of the 1960s, Congress gave the FBI greater power to investigate and break up racketeering operations. An illegal business run by organized crime is called a racket; hence, the charge is called *racketeering*.

One type of racket involves illegal gambling operations, in which the game is portrayed as being fairly run but there are never any winners. In another type of racket, a group of criminals move in on legitimate businesses, demanding that business owners pay for so-called "protection" to make sure no harm comes to those businesses. Of course, any harm would be the work of the racketeers themselves if the business owner did not go along with these criminals.

This type of bullying is a form of extortion. In the case of a small clothing firm, a fire or a major theft might hit the business. A member of the racketeers' organization would have set the fire or committed the theft. These "unfortunate incidents" would occur because the legitimate business owner refused to give in to the racketeers' demands. Sometimes, corrupt public officials might be on the racketeers' payroll as well. That way, even if a business owner complained to police, no action would be taken.

Nixon's Anti-Corruption Initiative
. . . and Watergate

During the late 1960s, the administration of President Richard M. Nixon urged federal law enforcement agencies

Richard Nixon (right) and Spiro Agnew are shown shortly after their election as U.S. president and vice president in 1968. Agnew resigned in disgrace in October 1973 after being charged with accepting bribes while holding public office. Less than a year later—in August 1974—Nixon would also resign in the middle of one of the most infamous public corruption scandals of all time—Watergate.

such as the FBI, the Department of Justice, and the U.S. Attorney's Office to spend substantially more money on fighting corruption on the local, state, and federal levels. This was the biggest anti-corruption initiative ever undertaken by the federal government up to that point.

Ironically—and unfortunately—during the early 1970s President Nixon himself became involved in a major public corruption case. In that case, known today as the Watergate scandal, the FBI and other federal agencies investigated acts of public corruption committed by the Nixon administration itself. What they discovered forced President Nixon to resign his office in disgrace.

In the early morning hours of June 17, 1972, five men were arrested for breaking into the Democratic National Committee headquarters in the Watergate hotel and office complex in Washington, D.C. They were caught photographing documents. Soon it became known that all five men had ties to Nixon's Committee to Re-Elect the President, also known as CREEP. Within days, the Nixon White House began covering up the break-in. The FBI was one of many government agencies that investigated the break-in and subsequent scandals, including campaign contribution irregularities and obstruction of justice involving some of Nixon's closest advisors.

Fallout from Watergate

The Watergate investigations led to **indictments** of many key Nixon White House officials, and Nixon himself resigned from office on August 8, 1974, over the scandal. In addition, Watergate prompted changes in election campaign financing laws, as well as the disclosures government officials are now required to make about where their money comes from. Watergate became the FBI's largest investigation since the assassination of President John F. Kennedy in 1963. In all, 300 agents and 51 FBI field offices took part in the Watergate probe.

After Watergate, a major change occurred in the way the FBI conducted investigations. This change was begun with little fanfare, but it included a crackdown on public corruption. In 1977, under the administration

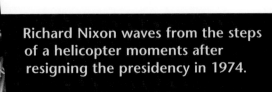

Richard Nixon waves from the steps of a helicopter moments after resigning the presidency in 1974.

of President Jimmy Carter, the FBI was granted the power to conduct sting operations. This revolutionized the way the FBI could conduct public corruption investigations.

"Stinging" Corrupt Public Officials

Until this change in policy, FBI agents could not pretend to be involved in a criminal activity in order to catch perpetrators committing a crime. With the change, the FBI became the only federal law enforcement agency allowed to use stings, and the stings had to be approved by officials throughout the FBI structure. The objective of these stings was to show public officials that (1) the FBI was taking an aggressive approach to public corruption; (2) the Bureau was creating an environment in which corrupt public servants would be identified, investigated, and prosecuted; and (3) corruption would not be tolerated in the public sphere.

William French Smith, who was attorney general under President Ronald Reagan, once told of how important it was for the FBI to use stings. He said the FBI had "to interject its agents into the midst of corrupt transactions. It must **feign** the role of corrupt participant. It must go underground."

Despite the FBI's tough stance on corruption, the agency also recognized that investigating charges of public corruption was an extremely sensitive matter. Irreversible damage could be done to a public official's career if the charges of public corruption were false or could not be proved.

Laying the Groundwork

Before beginning any probe, FBI officials make sure the charges call for an investigation. The Bureau is fully aware that if an investigation is launched on unfounded charges—

and if word of that investigation should become public—the public might assume the official is guilty solely because an investigation is underway.

With that in mind, the FBI gathers evidence—written and photographic documents or eyewitness testimony—to support any charges before an investigation is started. Officials try to determine whether an allegation is politically motivated or made out of bias—based, for example, on the official's race or religion. The agency must also guard against launching an investigation based on the claims of someone who might be angry or looking for

IT STINGS!

Usually when an insect stings people, it takes them by surprise. You might say they never saw it coming. The same could be said of undercover law enforcement operations, called *stings*.

When a law enforcement official or, with the consent of law enforcement, a member of the public pretends to play a role in a criminal enterprise to gather evidence against a suspected criminal, that investigation is called a sting. Stings are often used to catch people selling drugs, trading in weapons, or taking bribes. Stings are conducted in cases where gathering evidence would be difficult or even impossible if someone were not working undercover on behalf of law enforcement.

Law enforcement officers have to follow many rules when they're conducting a sting, including having a convincing reason to believe that the person or persons being investigated are involved in criminal activity in the first place. In a sting operation, officials must be careful not to do anything to provoke or force the targets of the investigation to commit a crime they would not otherwise commit. If this is done (a practice known as *entrapment*), there is a strong possibility that the case against the suspect would not hold up in court.

Before FBI agents can launch a sting operation, they must receive approval from Bureau supervisors and sometimes the courts. Once approved, however, these investigations are so secretive that, until arrests are made, the suspects have no idea they are about to be stung.

revenge against another person. The credibility of the entire FBI is at stake in each investigation the agency undertakes, and that credibility is greatly damaged if the agency pursues an unfounded investigation, motivated by politics, hate, or personal **animosity**.

So before agreeing to conduct a public corruption investigation, the FBI seeks to determine if a public official—whether elected or appointed—has committed an abuse of power or a **breach** of the public trust. At times, a sting is used to establish this pattern. That was the case in September 1978, when the FBI embarked on a widespread undercover operation known as Abscam.

Abscam: Posing as Middle Easterners

The FBI targeted federal and state public officials in the Abscam sting to see if those officials would accept bribes in exchange for providing political favors. FBI agents posed as businessmen from the Middle East. They claimed they were in charge of a business called Abdul Enterprises Ltd. The business was actually created by the FBI just for this sting operation.

The sting lasted until February 1980, when a story about the investigation broke on the NBC Nightly News. By the time the story came to light, corrupt officials had accepted more than $400,000 in bribes from Abdul Enterprises.

One U.S. senator—Harrison A. Williams (D-New Jersey)— and five members of the House of Representatives were found guilty of taking the bribes. The House members were from New Jersey, Pennsylvania, South Carolina, and Florida. Williams and four of the House members resigned from office, but one representative, Michael "Ozzie" Myers (D-Pennsylvania), had to be expelled from office by his colleagues. Also convicted in connection with the sting were five other lesser-known government officials, including a state senator from New Jersey and members of the Philadelphia City Council.

Abscam was the biggest corruption investigation of members of Congress to that point in U.S. history. Although the results of Abscam were generally hailed in public, people also raised some serious questions about techniques used by the FBI during the investigation.

This shot from a hidden FBI video surveillance camera shows U.S. Representative Michael Myers receiving an envelope containing $50,000 in bribes from FBI agents posing as Middle Eastern businessmen. Myers was expelled from Congress for his crimes.

Concerns about Entrapment and More

Many members of the public, the legal community, and Congress itself claimed that the FBI had entered uncharted territory with the Abscam sting. Some critics voiced concerns about entrapment (where an undercover law enforcement official lures someone into an illegal activity), violations of civil rights, and privacy issues.

FAST FACTS

The term *Abscam* comes from *Abdul Enterprises* Ltd., the name of the fake corporation set up by the FBI to *scam*, or trick, corrupt politicians into accepting bribes.

Some also questioned whether the FBI—or any law enforcement agency—should be allowed to devise an illegal activity and seek out prospective wrongdoers to participate in it. Was there not enough public corruption going on, these critics asked, without having to invent more?

For years following Abscam, these concerns led several U.S. attorneys general to revise the guidelines for the use of stings. In fact, this investigative tool is still being refined. Most officials agree, however, that the need for tough FBI investigations into public corruption—with or without stings—is crucial, because public corruption costs taxpayers serious money.

In June 2005 Supervisory Special Agent Dan O'Brien, then chief of the FBI's Public Corruption and Government Fraud program, said this about the cost of corruption to taxpayers:

When Senator Larry Pressler refused the bribes offered him by FBI undercover agents in the Abscam sting, CBS News hailed him as "a hero."

The Government Accountability Office estimates that at least 10 percent of the funding for federal government programs is lost to public corruption and government fraud each year. We're talking tens of billions of dollars.

As the number of public corruption cases continues to increase, the FBI has positioned itself as the firewall between the public trust and those seeking to destroy it.

JUST AN HONEST GUY

Larry Pressler was already a lawyer, a Vietnam veteran, and an experienced Foreign Service officer with the U.S. State Department when he decided to seek public office. A native of South Dakota, he represented his state as a Republican in the U.S. House of Representatives from 1975 to 1979 and in the U.S. Senate from 1979 to 1997. Pressler gained national and even international fame as the only member of Congress to refuse when offered a bribe in the Abscam scandal.

Unaware that the FBI was running the sting, Pressler turned down the bribe and then reported the entire incident to the Bureau. The FBI, which taped its encounter with each of the public officials approached in the scandal, even has Pressler on videotape turning down the bribe offer.

TV newscasts showed the tape of Pressler declining the bribe boldly and without hesitation, and his story made the front page of all the nation's major newspapers. Meanwhile, Pressler was taken aback by all the words of praise, especially the ones showered on him by renowned CBS News anchorman Walter Cronkite, who called Pressler a hero. Pressler, who had seen heroic acts in war, brushed off the reference, stating, "I do not consider myself a hero . . . What have we come to if turning down a bribe is 'heroic'?"

4 And Now for the Payoff

Public corruption is a difficult crime to detect. That is why the FBI relies heavily on tips from the public in order to learn about and battle corruption. Brave members of the public—sometimes at their own risk—come forward and tell the FBI about corruption that is going on in their community or even at the state and national levels.

Most public corruption occurs between individuals, with money often changing hands in private. Transactions taking place on such a personal level can be difficult to detect. If one of the people has misgivings or is unhappy with the payoff, however, that person may go from being a party to a crime to a tipster by making just one call to the FBI.

A Growing Intolerance for Corruption

Between 2004 and 2006, more than 1,000 corrupt public officials were convicted of crimes as a result of investigations conducted by the FBI, many with the help of tips from the public. In April 2008, the FBI reported more than 2,500 federal, state, and local investigations into public corruption that were being actively pursued. According to FBI Director Robert S. Mueller III, there would be even more if victims or witnesses to these crimes were not afraid to report what they knew to the FBI. Despite fears of **retribution**, however, Mueller has said, "There is a growing intolerance by the American people of public corruption—an intolerance reflected in the willingness to come forward and report abuse of public office."

With that in mind, the FBI has set up telephone hot lines and even a Web site for citizens to report corruption. If the person reporting the abuse wants to remain anonymous, the FBI honors that request.

Usually those reporting suspected corruption have some inside knowledge of what is going on. Most tipsters have been victims of a scam or have been asked to participate in the scam. Others have been asked to ignore the scam, or, in the course of their jobs, they have become aware of the scam because of accounting errors or financial shortfalls they have discovered.

Even people who may not have firsthand knowledge of wrongdoing, but simply suspect that corruption is going on, are encouraged to report their suspicions to

THANKS FOR THE TIP

Just watch the local news. If the police have a tough criminal case on their hands—a missing person, a hit-and-run, even a robbery at the local gas station—and they need your help, they set up a hot line for tips.

The same is true of the FBI, but in the case of corruption among public officials, the tip lines are open all the time. In addition, the FBI has a Web site where citizens can go online and give tips about possible corruption. Since 2006, the FBI has also had a Web site that has yielded valuable advice and tips on possible cases of public corruption, located at http://www.fbi.gov/hq/cid/pubcorrupt/pubcorrupt.htm. (See the sample screen shot from the Web site's home page below and to the right.) The idea for the Web site came from the Hurricane Katrina fraud site that brought in numerous solid leads on fraud-related crimes by people trying to make money off the Gulf Coast devastation.

Those submitting tips to the FBI corruption tip Web site can remain anonymous and provide as much information as they want. Of course, the more details they give the better, because it gives the Bureau more to work with when investigating each case. Since corruption cases take a long time to build, it may be a while before the FBI tracks down the lead and makes arrests, but all tips are taken seriously.

The FBI notes that not all cases make splashy headlines. While tips do lead to investigations and arrests, many cases don't make it into the news. But the point of the tips should be to stop corrupt government officials—nothing else.

Will your tip lead to an arrest? If it is solid and credible—and can be backed up with evidence—the FBI will follow it up with good old-fashioned legwork. That is what makes or breaks any case.

the FBI. Ongoing federal, state, and local investigations by the FBI focus on everything from government contracts that involve favoritism to unscrupulous campaign tactics. These might include voter fraud and questionable fund-raising practices. Many of the FBI's investigations started as tips from concerned people. And since most public corruption occurs in secret, most tips come from inside the government, from people who work there or deal with government officials.

Bribery: An Overview

So what kinds of public abuse does the FBI hear about from tipsters? The most common form of public corruption is the bribe (also known as a payoff). There have to be at least two parties involved in order for a bribe to take place. Usually, one person asks for the bribe and the other one pays it, or one person may offer the bribe and the second one will accept it. Sometimes more than one person may receive the bribe and more than one person may pay it. If one party **solicits** the bribe and the other pays, both are committing a crime.

Home | Site Map | FAQs

INVESTIGATION

SEARCH

Corruption

Report Corruption Now

Please contact us if you come across evidence of public corruption activities:
→ Submit an Online Tip
→ Call our Local Corruption Hotlines
- Katrina Fraud: (800) CALL FBI
- Birmingham, AL: (877) 628-2533
- Cincinnati, OH: (614) 744-2139
- Columbia, SC: (803) 551-4200
- Denver, CO: (888) 232-3270
- Knoxville, TN: (888) 678-6720
- Little Rock, AR: (501) 221-8200
- New York, NY: (877) 363-4723
- Puerto Rico: (877) FBI-SJPR
- Richmond, VA: (804) 627-4597
- Salt Lake City, UT: (866) 50-BRIBE
- San Diego, CA: (877) NO-BRIBE
- San Francisco, CA: (800) 376-5991
- Springfield, IL: (877) U-TIP-OFF
- U.S. Virgin Islands: (340) 774-9296
- More Local FBI Offices

- Inside School Corruption
- Election Crimes and the FBI
- More Stories

Recent Press Releases
- MA State Senator Indicted
- 15 IL Policemen Charged (pdf)
- AL Mayor Indicted in Bribery Scheme
- TX City Official Indicted for Bribery
- Virgin Islands Official Sentenced

If a public official agrees to take action on a matter in exchange for free season tickets to his favorite baseball team, that official is soliciting a bribe. A bribe could also be solicited by public officials in exchange for something they are already paid to do. For example, a federal official might approach a manufacturer who has followed the proper procedure in bidding on a contract with the government. The government official might demand a bribe before awarding the contract—even though the bidder followed all the rules and the contract should be awarded to the contractor who won it fair and square.

Treating a customer to courtside seats may be one way of building a good business relationship. It may also, however, be a way of influencing a politician's vote on a particular bill. In a case such as that, the seats may constitute a bribe.

Representative Randall "Duke" Cunningham of California pleaded guilty in November 2005 to taking more than $2.4 million in bribes from defense contractors. In exchange, Cunningham arranged for the contractors to get numerous government contracts and provided them with other political favors. The Cunningham case was investigated by the FBI following newspaper reports that the representative was involved in questionable real estate dealings with one of the defense contractors.

In court papers filed in connection with the case, Assistant U.S. Attorney Jason Forge wrote, "Cunningham demanded and received this money in return for being influenced in the performance of his official acts as a public official." Cunningham was sentenced to eight years and four months in prison. The FBI also investigated the contractors who gave the bribes to Cunningham and charged them with wrongdoing.

Bribery: Looking the Other Way

Bribes can also be solicited by public officials for doing something they are not supposed to do. In the case of former Representative Cunningham, the FBI found that he was using his influence to force government agencies to award jobs to the contractors who were giving him bribes, bypassing procedures normally followed for giving out such contracts.

Corrupt officials also solicit bribes to let local laws "slide." Say a homeowner wants to expand her house beyond the limits allowed by law. A corrupt building inspector may point out to the homeowner that the expansion request is prohibited by law—but he will allow it if the homeowner makes it worth his while to violate the law by giving him $1,000 to "look the other way."

FAST FACTS

The FBI claims it has never tried to track down a tipster who asked to remain anonymous.

U.S Representative Randall "Duke" Cunningham of California (left) is escorted out of federal court in November 2005 after pleading guilty to various corruption charges.

In both cases a government official is promising to look the other way, ignore the law, and fail to do his job if bribe money is paid. In exchange for a bribe, the public official will allow something to happen that breaks government rules set up for awarding contracts fairly, compromises the public safety, or violates the rights of members of the community.

Bribery: Swaying Government Decisions

A bribe may be offered or solicited so a public official will recommend something to other public officials or persuade them to vote a particular way. A public official may expect a bribe to use her influence to make certain things happen. For example, a city council member may solicit a bribe to agree to make sure that the person paying her off receives a contract to build a new school—a contract that person might not have otherwise won. Or that council member may solicit bribes from local restaurant owners to see that the council passes a bill prohibiting sidewalk vendors downtown, a law that council member might not otherwise have supported.

Bribes can also be used to get police officers to drop charges in traffic or criminal court or to get a judge to find a guilty defendant innocent.

Even hot dog stands require a license to operate. With so many interests competing for space and business, some restaurants might be tempted to offer local officials free food in exchange for granting a license—or for denying one to a competitor. Such a gift is a form of bribery.

Kickbacks: An Overview

The major difference between a bribe and a kickback is that a bribe is usually given before something happens and a kickback is usually given *after* something happens. Like a bribe, a kickback can be anything of value given in exchange for having corrupt public officials use their office or influence to get something done that would not have happened in the usual course of events.

For example, the mayor of a city allows a contractor to build more apartments on a piece of land than is allowed by law. The mayor uses his influence to get the city building inspector to approve the project and issue a **variance**. The mayor also gets the city council to go along with the project.

While the contractor is building the apartments, he puts a new wraparound porch on the mayor's house at no cost, and the mayor and his wife get a vacation to Greece, all expenses paid by the contractor. Once the project is completed, the mayor shares in some of the profits, and his brother gets one of the apartments for free or at a greatly reduced rent.

As with bribery, a kickback scheme requires more than one person. The mayor in the example just cited might have asked for the wraparound porch, the vacation, and the apartment for his brother, or the builder might have offered these things first. Yet neither was forced to agree to this illegal arrangement. Both parties would be guilty—unless one of them reports the kickbacks to the FBI. These kickbacks, which eat into the profits from a project, usually occur during or after the completion of the project. By contrast, a bribe is paid before any action is taken.

Extortion: An Overview

Extortion is a form of public corruption in which a public official demands a bribe or a kickback and threatens or actually uses violence to get it.

Here is one scenario that involves this nasty form of corruption: A public official in charge of purchasing office equipment waits until an office-supply company receives a contract to provide equipment at a set price. The official then asks the owner of the company for a kickback. When the contractor refuses to pay, the corrupt official threatens to hurt her family or blow up one of her trucks. That is extortion. If the public official hires some bullies to threaten to hurt her to show that he means business, that is extortion.

If the corrupt official carries out the threats, he can be charged with other crimes in addition to extortion. Because extortion is such a dangerous form of "persuasion," however, victims may be less likely to report it out of fear for their own safety and that of their families.

Graft, Embezzlement, Patronage

Another form of public corruption is graft. This refers to a large gift, usually something valued at more than $200, given

With many contracts to be awarded, building codes to be met, and regulations to be followed, construction projects give dishonest builders plenty of chances to offer bribes and kickbacks to corrupt public officials.

to a public official. Laws prohibit public officials from accepting large gifts while in office to avoid influencing their decisions, even if the gift is not intended to do that.

Embezzlement is the outright theft of money from the government. This includes everything from taking money out of a petty cash drawer to making out government checks to yourself for money that is not yours and that you have not earned. Embezzling funds can involve one person or many people.

FAST FACTS

Within three years of the terrorist attacks of September 11, 2001, more than 150,000 people applied to become special agents with the FBI. Only 2,200 of those applicants measured up to the Bureau's tough hiring standards, however, and were actually put on the job.

The FBI also investigates patronage charges, but not all patronage is against the law. Patronage occurs when a public official hires his supporters for government jobs, rather than someone else who is equally or better qualified. For a newly elected official to have his policies carried out, he needs to have supporters on the job. Patronage only crosses the line to become illegal when an incompetent or unqualified person is given a job over a qualified person, or a supporter is given a so-called "no-show" job for which she is paid and never has to come to work.

Once FBI agents know for certain that public corruption is going on, it's time to go get the bad guys.

CHAPTER

5 Gotcha!!!

The press release sounded all too familiar:

Washington D.C., September 26, 2007—A federal jury in Anchorage, Alaska, has found former Alaska State Representative and former Alaska Speaker of the House Peter Kott guilty of bribery, extortion, and conspiracy.

Kott was convicted of taking bribes to support an oil tax law favored by executives of VECO, a pipeline service and construction company. He was not the only state representative convicted in connection with the scandal and not the only public official the FBI investigated in the case. By far the best-known political figure in the VECO case was then-U.S. Senator

Before his conviction on corruption charges and defeat in the November 2008 election, Senator Ted Stevens of Alaska had been the longest-serving Republican in the U.S. Senate.

Ted Stevens. Following his conviction in October 2008 on several corruption charges, Stevens lost a close election to Mark Begich in November. Prior to that loss, Stevens had been a U.S. senator from Alaska since 1968.

Corruption on the Rise?

With more public corruption cases pending than ever before, and over 620 FBI agents and all 56 field offices working on public corruption cases, it is clear that the FBI is following through on its pledge to make public corruption a top priority. FBI Director Robert S. Mueller III has said that he does not believe there is more public corruption now than in the past. Instead, the FBI's special agents appear to be more adept at investigating and rooting out corruption.

Public corruption investigations by the FBI have been conducted in every state. No state has an unblemished record when it comes to public corruption. Here are a few examples of cases involving public officials who violated their oaths of office.

Pardons for Sale

In the late 1970s, the FBI was called in to handle a wide-ranging corruption scheme in Tennessee involving officials selling prison pardons for up to $10,000 each. The investigation of this scheme exposed a member of the Tennessee state police as well as several aides of then-Governor Ray Blanton. Two of Blanton's aides were convicted in connection with the scandal, but Blanton himself was never charged in that case. He did, however, spend 22 months in prison on separate charges related to the sale of liquor licenses while in office.

Operation Greylord

People turn to the judicial system when they are victimized. They don't expect law enforcement officers or members of the judicial system, such as judges, to be involved in crime themselves. Corruption by these officials is among of the most serious and outrageous of all public corruption violations.

In the 1980s, the FBI undertook an extensive investigation into traffic ticket fixing in Chicago. At the center of the investigation was Harold Conn, the deputy traffic court clerk in Cook County, Illinois, who served as the bagman, or courier, for the operation. Conn was convicted of taking bribes that he later used to buy off judges to drop or reduce traffic charges, a practice known as fixing tickets. Operation Greylord, named after the curly wigs British judges wear, netted 92 corrupt officials.

The corrupt officials included 17 judges and 48 lawyers as well as a state legislator, police officers, court officials, and deputy sheriffs. Many pleaded guilty; most of the others were convicted in one of the biggest investigations of the judicial system ever. To catch the crooked officials, the FBI set up a sting operation with the help of honest judges and lawyers

Deputy traffic court clerk Harold Conn, shown here in the top row, center photo, was also at the center of the dozens of officials ensnared in the FBI's Operation Greylord bribery sting in Chicago.

posing as corrupt officials. The operation put an end to judicial corruption that local officials claimed had gotten so out of hand they just didn't have the resources to stop it themselves.

Operation Pretense

One of Mississippi's biggest corruption scandals exposed 57 of the 410 county supervisors in the state and was brought to light by the FBI's Operation Pretense. The case involved so many public officials and such widespread **malfeasance** that it even got the attention of *60 Minutes*, the popular CBS newsmagazine program. The exhaustive FBI undercover investigation unearthed a complex and devious purchasing system, controlled by the county supervisors and supported by fake documentation.

The FBI's investigation started in 1984. Shortly before that, John Burgess, a minister, invested in a pipe manufacturing business near Jackson, Mississippi. Sales representatives at the company told him one day that they had to kick back money (usually 10 percent of each sale) to county supervisors or the supervisors would not do business with the company. The minister reported this to the FBI.

After some preliminary investigation, the FBI asked the minister to work undercover to set up a front, or bogus, company to help trap the corrupt officials. In fact, Operation Pretense stands for the "Preacher's Ten-Percent Supervisors Expense." Burgess used a hidden microphone (known as a wire) to tape the county supervisors as they asked him for kickbacks on any business they gave him.

Supervisors basically ran the show in these Mississippi counties when it came to purchasing any government supplies. They made the purchase, signed receipts specifying that they got the items, and authorized, or approved, payment. No other government officials were involved, so covering up corruption was relatively easy.

Once they saw how the scheme worked, the FBI took over most of the undercover work and continued the investigation for several years. When the investigation came to an end, all but one of the supervisors either pleaded guilty or was convicted of taking kickbacks. Some of the supervisors faced other criminal charges as well, including bribery and extortion. Most went to prison. One county road foreman, two state highway commissioners, and 13 vendors were also convicted of public corruption in this case.

John Burgess, the minister who first reported on the corrupt officials to the FBI, received the Louis E. Peters Memorial Award in 1991. This award, presented each year by the Society of Former Special Agents of the FBI, is named after a brave California businessman who helped the FBI expose members of organized crime who were trying to move in on his business. Wayne R. Taylor, special agent in charge of the

FAST FACTS

Corporatecrimereporter.com reported in October 2007 that 20,000 public officials and private citizens over the previous 20 years had been convicted of public corruption, according to U.S. Justice Department data.

FBI in Mississippi at the time of Operation Pretense, said that the award is given to

> . . . a citizen who at great personal sacrifice gave unselfishly of themselves to serve their community and nation [and] . . . stood up and said, "This is not right, and I can do something about it."

Battling Bribery

Another brave citizen, Robert Rieser, the director of public works for the city of Aurora, Illinois, earned the prestigious Louis E. Peters Memorial Award as well. In January 2004, a former city alderman approached Rieser and offered him a bribe to allow a land developer to build on a 7-acre (2.8-hectare) piece of land that had extreme flooding problems.

Rieser reported the bribery attempt to the mayor, who turned the matter over to the FBI. The FBI started an investigation and asked Rieser to help gather hard evidence to prove the allegations. It was a tough mission for Rieser because the former city alderman was also his friend, but the public well-being was at stake. Rieser said he needed "to do the right thing, no matter what the cost may be." During the course

Robert Rieser (fourth from left) is shown accepting an award from FBI Director Robert S. Mueller. Other past and present FBI agents and leaders joined Mueller to honor Rieser for his stand against public corruption as a city official in Aurora, Illinois.

of the investigation, evidence was also uncovered showing that while he was in office the former city alderman had accepted bribes from the land developer. He was eventually indicted, based on the hard work by both the FBI and Rieser.

The former alderman pleaded guilty to the charges; the land developer was also charged and found guilty in court. A statement released by the FBI in 2005, when Rieser received his award, said of the award winner, "There are few men who will stand up for what is right and even fewer when it comes at the cost of their personal safety or relationships."

Operation Tennessee Waltz

In May 2002, the FBI began a **landmark** corruption investigation that became known as Operation Tennessee Waltz. Starting on the local level, with public officials in some Tennessee towns, the case grew to include state officials as well.

Special agents of the FBI posed as representatives of a fake company that disposed of outdated electronics equipment and asked elected officials to support legislation that would promote the company's interest and help them receive a contract to acquire and dispose of the equipment. The legislators agreed, but they asked for bribes in return for their votes. The bribes ranged from $2,500 to $55,000 apiece.

The case ended with the conviction or guilty pleas of numerous Tennessee public officials in 2006 and 2007. It also prompted sweeping **reforms** in the state's **ethics** laws. The investigation led to the arrest of seven state lawmakers as well as a number of county officials and two local Tennessee school board members.

A suspect in the Tennessee Waltz case is caught on tape by a hidden FBI surveillance camera. He is speaking with an undercover agent posing as a representative of a fake company that has offered Tennessee officials bribes in exchange for a lucrative business deal.

Selling Licenses and More

In 2006, former Illinois Governor George Ryan was convicted on 18 charges, including taking bribes and racketeering. The FBI claimed that Ryan, who had been governor from 1999 to 2003 and Illinois secretary of state from 1991 to 1999, had made it clear that his office was for sale.

The FBI investigation started when agents began looking into complaints that Ryan was selling driver's licenses to unqualified truck drivers while he was secretary of state. From that investigation came evidence of bribe taking and other crimes while he was governor. A total of 79 people—many state workers—were charged in connection with the scandal surrounding Ryan.

The Abramoff Scandal

In January 2006, Jack Abramoff pleaded guilty to corruption charges in a scandal that rocked Washington, D.C., and Republican politics to its core. Abramoff was one of Washington's most influential and respected lobbyists. The FBI found that Abramoff and his lobbying partners had extorted money from the operators of Native American tribal

UNSAFE AT ANY LEVEL

Public corruption is about greed, but it is also about where greed can lead.

Public corruption is not limited to elected officials. People who are appointed to and hired for government jobs may also be involved in public corruption if they violate the trust placed in them. Corruption by trusted government workers can cut right to the core of some of the nation's key concerns. One of the major concerns today is national security.

Employees at motor vehicle agencies all over the country now hold some of the government's most important jobs. They are in charge of giving out driver's licenses, which today are considered the most legitimate form of official identification in the United States. Driver's licenses are used as ID (identification) for everything from cashing checks to getting on airplanes. A department of motor vehicles worker who accepts a bribe to issue a fraudulent driver's license opens the door to many types of illegal acts by the license holder, including getting past security at public events, transportation hubs, and government buildings.

Since the terror attacks of 9/11, these checkpoints have been set up to protect all U.S. residents and to head off future attacks. All a terrorist needs to penetrate security is a valid ID, so giving out a fake driver's license means much more than taking a bribe to put an illegal driver on the road—it can undermine national security.

In July 2003, the FBI arrested two Virginia Department of Motor Vehicles employees, among others, charging them with making and selling state driver's licenses. The scam, which was broken through a sting called Operation Easy Rider, produced more than 1,000 illegal licenses. That is why the FBI says public corruption is dangerous at any level.

The importance of driver's licenses as a form of ID has given motor vehicle departments, such as the one shown here, a significant role in the fight against public corruption.

The probe into Jack Abramoff's illicit business dealings in Washington, D.C., also led to the investigation of numerous public officials. These included members of the Bush administration and Congressional lawmakers and staff members.

gambling concerns in exchange for representing their interests in Washington. Those interests actually needed little representation, and Abramoff instead used the money to buy influence with high-level Washington Republicans for other purposes that would benefit him.

Once Abramoff pleaded guilty to the corruption charges, a number of notable Republicans, such as Representative Tom DeLay (R-Texas), House Speaker Dennis Hastert (R-Illinois), and Senate Majority Leader Bill Frist (R-Tennessee), quickly gave back donations they had accepted from him. For a variety of reasons, all three chose not to seek reelection in 2006.

One of those charged in connection with the scandal was Representative Bob Ney (R-Ohio). He pleaded guilty in October 2006 to charges related to bribery and to giving false statements about the Abramoff scandal. He resigned from office in November after already announcing his intention not to seek reelection. He was convicted of the charges against him and sent to prison. In August 2008, Ney was released from prison after serving 17 months of a 30-month sentence. Congressional aides have also been criminally charged in connection with the scheme.

Public Corruption— a Burden on the FBI and Democracy Alike

In a speech about the U.S. Constitution, former Vice President Al Gore had this to say:

> The Abramoff scandal is but the tip of a giant iceberg that threatens the integrity of the entire legislative branch of government.

FAST FACTS

In 2004 the FBI had 264 agents working on public corruption cases. That number continues to grow, reaching over 620 in 2008, with more agents being assigned all the time.

In his speech, Gore was concerned about the corruption that had reached the highest levels of the U.S. Congress. In his view, however, another evil of public corruption is that it also provides an excuse to the government to spy on the lives of ordinary citizens as well as elected officials.

The FBI's investigations into corrupt public officials—and the resulting convictions and resignations—have brought the subject of public corruption more into the public eye than ever before. As evidenced in the 2008 elections, candidates are coming under closer scrutiny for their ties with lobbyists and others who might attempt to influence lawmakers. Of course, close attention by the media and voters alone cannot guarantee that public officials will remain honest and **above reproach** as they conduct the day-to-day business of government. That is why the FBI must be counted on to make sure the public trust is never violated or taken for granted.

CHRONOLOGY

1924: The Teapot Dome scandal comes to light. One of the earliest public corruption scandals investigated by the Bureau of Investigation (now the FBI), the scandal involved officials who illegally profited from the lease of government oil fields.

1972: On June 17, a break-in at the Democratic National Committee in Washington, D.C., by men with ties to President Richard Nixon launches the Watergate scandal.

1977: Foreign Corrupt Practices Act (FCPA) is passed in an effort to stop the bribing of public officials to win contracts with companies doing business with the United States.

1978: The FBI launches its Abscam sting, which lasts until February 1980, to see if federal and state officials would accept bribes in exchange for providing political favors.

1984: In Operation Greylord, Harold Conn, deputy traffic court clerk in Cook County, Illinois, is convicted of taking bribes to buy off judges to drop or reduce traffic charges.

The FBI starts Operation Pretense, an undercover investigation into dozens of corrupt Mississippi officials taking money from businesses in exchange for placing orders.

2002: U.S. Representative James A. Traficant, Jr. (D-Ohio) is found guilty of demanding bribes from business executives and taking kickbacks from his own staff.

The FBI begins Operation Tennessee Waltz, in which agents catch state officials willing to accept bribes in exchange for contracts.

The FBI begins undercover Operation Lively Sting, resulting in the arrests of nearly 70 U.S. military and law enforcement members on corruption charges in the smuggling of illegal drugs, drug money, and immigrants from Mexico into the United States.

2005: On August 29, Hurricane Katrina causes massive damage to New Orleans and other Gulf Coast areas. In September, the FBI sets up a tip line to help combat the misuse of relief funds being poured into the area.

U.S. Representative Randall "Duke" Cunningham (R-California) pleads guilty to taking bribes from defense contractors in exchange for lucrative government contracts.

2006: Prominent Washington lobbyist Jack Abramoff pleads guilty to corruption charges, including defrauding Native American tribes that were his own clients.

Former Illinois Governor George Ryan is convicted on corruption charges, including taking bribes and racketeering.

2008: After serving 40 years in the U.S. Senate, Ted Stevens of Alaska is found guilty of corruption charges in a case involving an oil construction firm. He loses his seat to Mark Begich in the November election.

2009: In January, the Illinois House votes to impeach Governor Rod Blagojevich on charges of fraud and misconduct. The Illinois Senate tries him on those charges and votes to remove him from office. In April, a federal grand jury indicts him on criminal conspiracy charges.

GLOSSARY

above reproach—incapable of being criticized; perfect.

animosity—ill will or bad feelings.

breach—violation, as of the public trust.

censure—an official expression of disapproval or condemnation of a person who has violated laws or established procedures.

coercion—attempting to persuade someone to do something by using threats or violence.

condone—to overlook something although one knows it is wrong.

conflict of interest—a situation in which one's public responsibilities and private interests may compete. For example, a judge whose daughter is on trial would find that his desire to keep her out of jail would compete with his duty to be fair and impartial.

Constitution—a written document, in effect since 1789, outlining the basic laws and values by which the United States is governed.

corruption—behaving dishonestly or fraudulently, particularly from a position of power.

cronies—friends; partners in crime.

dictatorship—a form of government in which all the nation's political and military power is in the hands of one person or a small group who have either seized power or, once elected, refused to let others challenge them in free and open elections.

embezzle—to take funds illegally from an organization or institution; usually done by someone working for that organization.

ethics—having to do with morality or the idea of right vs. wrong.

extortion—attempting to get a bribe or kickback by means of violence or the threat of violence.

feign—to pretend, or put on a false front.

indictments—official charges, against an individual or an organization, which often lead to a trial.

kickbacks—a form of public corruption in which a person or company gives back ("kicks back") money to someone else in exchange for something of value, such as a business contract.

landmark—of historic significance; an event that marks a change or turning point in something.

malfeasance—deliberate wrongdoing.

money laundering—moving money through several banks or businesses to conceal the fact it was gained by committing crimes.

pardon—in law, to forgive a convicted criminal for his or her crime; includes releasing an offender from the legal consequences of having been convicted of a crime. Pardons are often granted by government executives, such as governors and presidents.

patronage—giving or receiving a political job based on a person's political connections.

racketeering—a form of public corruption involving organized illegal activity, often in business dealings.

recrimination—an accusation made in response to an initial accusation or some other insult.

reform—to improve something, usually socially or politically, often by removing inefficient, corrupt, or dishonest practices.

reprisal—an act in response to another (usually harmful) act.

retribution—punishment for doing something harmful to another.

scam—a scheme or trick designed to fool someone, usually for the purpose of getting money.

solicit—to ask for something, as a bribe.

undermine—to weaken.

unscrupulous—not restrained by moral or ethical principles.

variance—permission to vary from local law in connection with building roads or structures.

FURTHER READING

Abagnale, Frank W., and Stan Redding. *Catch Me if You Can: The True Story of a Real Fake*. New York: Broadway Books, 2000.

Crockett, James R. *Operation Pretense: The FBI's Sting on County Corruption in Mississippi*. Jackson: University Press of Mississippi, 2003.

Douglas, John, and Mark Olshaver. *The Anatomy of a Motive*. reprint edition. New York: Pocket Books, 2000.

Fisher, David. *Hard Evidence: How Detectives Inside the FBI's Sci-Crime Lab Have Helped Solve America's Toughest Cases*. New York: Simon & Schuster, 1995.

Holden, Henry M. *FBI 100 Years: An Unofficial History*. Minneapolis: Zenith Press, 2008.

INTERNET RESOURCES

http://www.fbi.gov
The official site of the FBI includes the latest information about public corruption as well as archives about past cases of official misconduct.

http://www.usdoj.gov
The Department of Justice site has press releases about public officials who have been indicted for committing crimes while in office. The site also contains information and updates about pending cases against public officials.

http://www.icac.nsw.gov.au/
The site of the Independent Commission Against Corruption focuses on corruption on an international scale.

http://www.irs.gov/compliance/index.html
The site of the Internal Revenue Service includes articles and press releases regarding public officials charged by the IRS with criminal activities in connection with their public office.

http://www.corporatecrimereporter.com
This online newsletter contains stories and information about public corruption as well as corporate corruption. Updated regularly.

**http://www.lawyershop.com/practice-areas/criminal-law/
white-collar-crimes/public-corruption/**
The public corruption page of LawyerShop.com has the latest news about public corruption.

The Web sites mentioned in this book were active at the time of publication. The publisher is not responsible for Web sites that have changed their addresses or discontinued operation since the date of publication. The publisher will review and update the Web site addresses each time the book is reprinted.

NOTES

Chapter 1

p. 8: "scared to death of my . . .": Francis X. Clines, "Ohio Congressman Guilty in Bribery and Kickbacks," *New York Times* (April 12, 2002), http://query.nytimes.com/gst/fullpage.html?res=9907E3D7173CF931A25757C0A9649C8B63.

p. 8: "A member of Congress . . .": Ibid.

p. 9: "Unless a man is honest . . .": Theodore Roosevelt, "The Eighth and Ninth Commandments in Politics," *Outlook* (May 12, 1900), www.bartleby.com/58/7.html.

p. 10: "our highest criminal priority . . .": "Bribes Beyond the Border: Stemming the Export of Corruption," Federal Bureau of Investigation (February 5, 2007), http://www.fbi.gov/page2/feb07/fcpa020507.htm.

p. 11: "companies should thrive . . .": Ibid.

p. 12: "The FBI is uniquely situated . . .": "Major Executive Speeches," Federal Bureau of Investigation (April 17, 2008), http://www.fbi.gov/pressrel/speeches/mueller041708.htm.

p. 13: "For a nation built . . .": Ibid.

p. 13: "If you would sell your oath . . .": Ibid.

Chapter 2

p. 15: "We have a responsibility to ensure that government relief efforts . . .": "FBI Announces Tip Line to Combat Public Corruption & Government Fraud," Federal Bureau of Investigation (September 15, 2005), http://www.fbi.gov/pressrel/pressrel05/pr091505.htm.

p. 24: "Let the guilty be punished . . ." Nathan Miller, *New World Coming: The 1920s and the Making of Modern America* (New York: Scribner, 2003), p. 126.

Chapter 3

p. 30: "to interject its agents . . ." David Burnham, "The F.B.I.: A Special Report," *The Nation* (August 11, 1997), http//trac.syr.edu/tracreports/archive/reportnation970811.html.

p. 35: "The Government Accountability Office estimates . . ." "Cracking Down on Public Corruption: Why We Take It So Seriously . . . and Why It Matters to You," Federal Bureau of Investigation (June 20, 2005), http://www.fbi.gov/page2/june05/obrien062005.htm.

p. 35: "I do not consider . . ." Larry Pressler, quoted in "In the News–Some Highlights," SenatorLarryPressler.com (undated), http://www.senatorlarrypressler.com/biography.html.

Chapter 4

p. 37: "There is a growing intolerance . . ." Seth Hettena, "FBI establishes Website to collect tips on public corruption," found in SFGate (May 11, 2006), http://www.sfgate.com/cgibin/article.cgi?f=/n/a/2006/05/11/state/n163445D78.DTL&type.

p. 40: "Cunningham demanded and received . . ." Onell R. Soto, "Cunningham 'Demanded and Received' Bribe, Prosecutors Say," *San Diego Union-Tribune* (August 25, 2005), http://www.signonsandiego.com/news/politics/20050825-1640-bn24duke.html.

Chapter 5

p. 46: "Washington D.C., September 26, 2007 . . ." "Former Alaska State Speaker of the House Peter Kott Convicted on Public Corruption Charges," Federal Bureau of Investigation–Anchorage Field Division–Department of Justice Press Release (September 26, 2007). http://anchorage.fbi.gov/doj/pressrel/2007/publiccorruption092507.htm

p. 51: "a citizen who at great . . .": James R. Crockett, *Operation Pretense: The FBI's Sting on County Corruption in Mississippi* (Jackson: University of Mississippi Press, 2003), p. 5.

p. 51: "to do the right thing . . .": "Extraordinary Public Service Honored: Spotlight on Robert Rieser," Federal Bureau of Investigation (November 7, 2005), http://www.fbi.gov/page2/nov05/publicservice110705.htm.

p. 52: "There are few men . . .": Ibid.

p. 56: "The Abramoff scandal is but the tip of a giant . . .": "Transcript: Former Vice President Gore's Speech on Constitutional Issues,": *Washington Post* (January 16, 2006), http://www.washingtonpost.com/wp-dyn/content/article/2006/01/16/AR2006011600779.html.

INDEX

About the Author

Robert Grayson is an award-winning former daily newspaper reporter, and the author of a book of crime victims' services called the *Crime Victim's Aid*. Among the hundreds of articles he has written are pieces on the judicial system, including "Criminal Justice Vs. Victim Justice: A Need to Balance the Scales," published in the *Justice Reporter*. Throughout his journalism career, Robert has written stories on sports, arts and entertainment, business, pets, and profiles. His work has appeared in national and regional publications.